Speed Learning Graphology ~
The Art Of Handwriting Analysis

Julian Moore

www.thecoldreadingcompany.co.uk

Speed Learning Graphology ~ The Art Of Handwriting Analysis

Amazon Print Edition

To download the ten free flash cards that accompany this text please see the link at the back of the book

You can download the FREE audiobook of this text over at http://thecoldreadingcompany.co.uk - just look for the 'free audiobook' link

Contents

INTRODUCTION

It's not hard to argue that people's handwriting style says something about their personality. From the slapdash but speedy scrawling of the impassioned English student to the small but perfectly formed geometry of the architect's signature, everybody is reflected in their handwriting to at least a certain degree.

Because of this, graphology or 'handwriting analysis' is taken more seriously than similar personality readings as people feel it has a more scientific grounding based on the actions and life decisions of an individual. Other personality reading types such as palmistry tend to work less well in a more formal environment but, just like the palm of the hand, everyone has a handwriting style and a signature, and everyone want's to know more about themselves.

Just because graphology has a foot in science doesn't mean that handwriting analysis can't be fun though. Handwriting analysis works best in groups as everyone can compare styles, and there is less worry from one person to the next that they may be giving away a personal secret. It is, after all, just handwriting.

Over the years I have collected a variety of graphology and handwriting analysis books. There is a vast amount of information which is very easy to forget and almost impossible to explain to another human being without boring them to death.

The aim of this book is to describe a very simple, fun and easy to remember graphology method to give quick readings of about ten minutes to an individual or a group.

Hopefully it is memorable enough so that not only can you remember it extremely quickly, but the people you do it for can remember it as well. I am a great believer that in all types of personality readings, if you teach what you preach you will never be forgotten.

Before we start, here is a little rhyme that you may have heard before. Do you know what it's about?

One for sorrow,

two for joy,

three for a girl,

four for a boy,

five for silver,

six for gold,

seven for a secret,

never to be told,

eight for a wish,

nine for a kiss,

ten for a time

of joyous bliss.

THE METHOD

The system is based on just two words written in **lower** case - 'two magpies'. These two words have been picked to include some of the most useful letters of the alphabet for graphology purposes, and to create a memorable image. Having only two words to write cuts down the time it takes those participating to get involved, and is also easier to write less when one is standing up. It also means that you can do an analysis on the back of a business card.

two magpies

The magpie nursery rhyme also serves as a great backstory and introduction, as well as bringing people luck - 'two for joy'. There are even ten letters in the phrase - and ten is for 'joyous bliss'. So by simply participating, your audience will feel like they're lucky. We also take a sample of their personal signature.

The letters are discussed in pairs as this greatly enhances the analysis.

Letter Pairings

The letter **G** and the letter **P** (the social and physical)

The letter **T** and the letter **I** (the drive and the finish)

The letter **W** and the letter **M** (the path one must tread)

The letter **O** and the letter **E** (the spoken and the heard)

The letter **A** and the letter **S** (cats and birds)

There is also **Style**, **Slant and Baselines** and the person's **Signature** to take into consideration.

With my method I have taken some very small liberties with the exact meanings of the letters as defined in the graphology literature, but I feel that it is worth it to give an interesting and memorable analysis.

1. G and P – Let's Get Physical

The letters G and P both have to do with the gregarious and the physical and as such it is appropriate that they both sit together in our 'two magpies' phrase.

Memory tip: Think 'Gregarious' for the G. Think 'Physical' for the P.

What we are looking at here are the size of the loops in the letters G and the P.

The bigger the loops, the more of that trait the person has. By comparing these two letters together we can come to some conclusions:

Small G loop / large P loop	Socially selective, could make up for it with physical activity
Large G loop / small P loop	Gregarious, may prefer to spend time socially rather than in physical activity
Small G loop / small P loop	Socially selective, not that physical, tends to be a loner

Small G loop / large P loop	Socially selective, could make up for it with physical activity
Large G loop / large P loop	Gregarious and physically active, probably enjoys team sports and social outings

If the loops are so tight that there is hardly any loop to them this can denote a shyer quieter type.

Comparing the size of the loops of the letters G and P can give you a lot of mileage and it is a good way to start a graphology reading as it is very simple process. However one should not only judge the loops against each other but also against the size of the overall writing.

This is especially true when the loops in both letters appear to be the same size.

G & P Recap

G loops show how gregarious someone is

P loops show how physical they are

Bigger loops - more

Smaller loops - less

* Top Tip: *Look to see if the loops are incomplete or end abruptly. This can indicate frustration socially and/or physically.*

* Top Tip: *If you are having problem judging the loops or there simply aren't any at all, judge the length of the stems.*

Additional notes

If you are entertaining a more adult crowd and want to break the ice, using the G for 'G-Spot' and bringing in some more sexual connotations can be great fun, especially as this encourages people to compare each others scribbles. This is still in keeping with modern graphology ideas. I'll leave it to your own imagination as to what the letter P could mean.

Exercise One

By just looking at the G and the P, can you match these samples with the descriptions below?

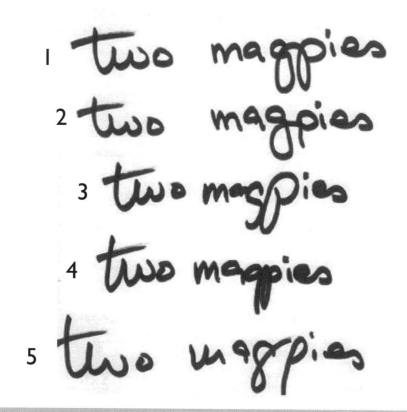

Answers: 1B:2C:3E:4D:5A

2. T and I – Let's Play Golf

The letter T is one of the most significant letters in graphology and is an indicator of ones overall demeanor. The letter I is similar but also brings with it the idea of precision and attainment.

By using these two letters together we have an indicator of how someone goes about achieving their goals and if they are successful.

In modern graphology the crossing of the T is said to show how someone approaches life:

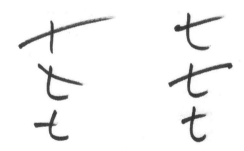

Also, the dotting of the I shows a person's attention to detail:

Reading into these letters can still be quite tricky and this is why I use something I call The Golf Analogy.

The Golf Analogy

By using The Golf Analogy with the letter T and the letter I in the phrase 'two magpies' the whole phrase becomes the fairway / golf course.

Imagine that the letter T represents the golfer and the crossing of the T represents his swing (easily remembered as this is the Tee Shot)

Imagine that the stem of the letter I represents the flag on the golfing green where the hole is.

Imagine that the the dot of the I represents the golf ball.

Whether you like golf or not, the way someone swings at the ball can tell us something about the way the golfer approaches life, and his accuracy in getting the ball near the hole (flag) shows us something about his ability to reach his goals.

Does he aim ridiculously high and overshoot? Or take a small but direct shot and get a hole in one? Does the ball miss the mark even though he hit the ball with great strength, or does it land very close to the flag against all odds after having been driven into the ground?

Examples

What can we say about this person in our imaginary game of golf?

From this handwriting sample, we can see a high and hard swing has overshot the hole considerably. This is likely to be someone who has a great deal of enthusiasm but often over-stretches himself.

This person on the other hand has taken a perfectly measured and straight shot and landed right on the flag. This denotes a person who takes quick decisive action and pays attention to detail.

This person has managed to get the ball on the flag even though he's driven it into the fairway. Probably someone who doesn't look too far ahead and doesn't have wild ambition, but gets what he wants eventually.

As you can see with these three examples, you can get quite a lot out of this analogy and it's great fun.

The Height Of The Dot

It is perfectly possible to have the dot of the I directly above the stem but still at some distance (height) from the main letter.

This still constitutes a 'hit' or 'hole in one' - however, the higher the dot is from the stem, the less the person is satisfied with their success and will still be yearning for higher things and further achievements.

* Top Tip: If there is no dot on the I at all we can assume that the ball is missing in the rough - the person is somewhat confused about where to put their energy and isn't quite sure where their goals lie!

T & I Recap (*Golf analogy*)
T = Tee shot
I = Flag/Hole
Dot of the i = golf ball
Swing (cross of the T) = approach
Accuracy (how well i is dotted) = attainment

Exercise Two

By looking at the T and the I ONLY, can you match these samples with the descriptions on the next page?

1 two magpies

2 two magpies

3 two magpies

4 two magpies

5 two magpies

6 two magpies

7 two magpies

8 Two magpies

9 two magpies

10 two magpies

A - Prepares well but doesn't see things through at all - his lofty ambitions tend to be realised so perhaps relies on other people

B - Although he takes a measured approach, he often goes too far - could do with loosening up a little perhaps

C - Has great confidence and foresight and is often able to set out what he planned to achieve

D - Extremely lofty ideals gets this person exactly where they want to be, but may well be over the heads of others

E - Tries to exert a fair level of control on his life, but still tends to try to hard

F - Tends to aim far too low but nevertheless arrives at his goals eventually

G - Doesn't set his sights at all high enough, but that isn't surprising as he is still to figure out what he wants

H - An extremely measured approach gets him what he wants although he is hardly ever satisfied

I - Starts well but fails to follow through so often doesn't reach his goals

J - Terrific get up and go which unfortunately often results in let down - someone who may be 'full of it'

3. W and M – Waves Mountains

The W and M are very similar letters and the way these letters are written in graphology give us an inkling into the way a person thinks.

The *flow* of someone's handwriting is mainly a stylistic interpretation and relates to how joined up and consistent the writing is. It can also be called *rhythm* - just like in music, you can see when someone writes a sentence whether there is a steady style running through it or if it's disjointed or broken into sections.

The letters W and M are particularly good for spotting this *rhythm* and *flow* as they consist entirely of up and down strokes.

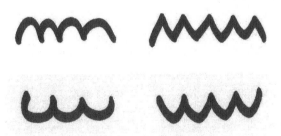

Because these letters are so easy to write, graphology tends to look at them as indicators of speed and depth of thought. The letters W and M therefore are fairly analogous to the concepts of peaks and troughs both in water and in mountains.

The Letter W - Water

I'm sure you've heard of the phrase 'still waters run deep' - well with the letter W for water this is largely true.

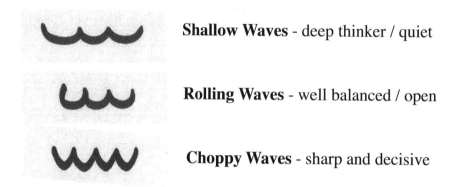

Shallow Waves - deep thinker / quiet

Rolling Waves - well balanced / open

Choppy Waves - sharp and decisive

Using the water analogy these are extremely easy to remember.

The Letter M - Mountains

With the letter M we also have some similar meanings, and it is helpful to think of the type of person who traverses each terrain:

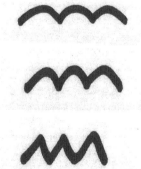

Meadows - walked by ramblers
     (broad thinking / takes his time)

Hills - climbed by hikers
     (steady thinking / gets things done)

Mountains - scaled by mountaineers
     (quick thinking / likes a challenge)

There are also two other things to notice about the way the M is written.

If the M is written slanting **Downwards** then the person is **Diplomatic** (would let someone **down** gently):

If the M is written slanting **Upwards** then the person is **Unconfident** (would never take the **upper** hand):

Apart from these last two ideas, the whole of the phrase should be looked at to give an overall indication of the flow and rhythm. However it is very rare that the style of the phrase will be much different than that of these two letters.

__Top Tip__: Sometimes a person's handwriting is so quick across the page as to be almost a single line or lightning bolt. These people are incredibly quick thinkers and often leave people behind with their indecipherable scrawls and sudden flashes of inspiration!

<u>W & M Recap</u>

W = Water

M = Mountains

Soft curves = slow, deep, broad thinking

Jagged peaks = sharp, quick, decisive thinking

Exercise Three

By looking at the W and the M ONLY, can you match these samples with their descriptions?

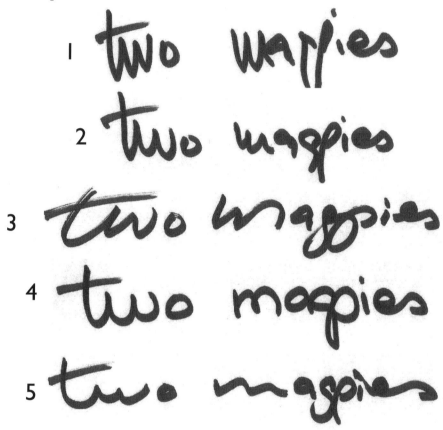

1 two magpies

2 two magpies

3 two magpies

4 two magpies

5 two magpies

A - Open steady thinker, but lacks confidence

B - Well balanced quick thinking diplomat

C - Quick thinker, sharp and decisive

D - Deep thinking time taking diplomat

E - Well balanced steady thinker

4. O and E – Mouth and Ears

The O and E are the mouth and ears of graphology and show us how someone communicates with and listens to the world around them.

Memory tip: The letter O is like a mouth, and E is for Ear.

The way a person talks and the way they listen are two important aspects of a person's personality. No one likes to hear someone drone on and on but at the same time it is nice to know when someone is actually listening to what you are saying. The O and the E show us these traits.

The Letter O

With the O you are looking to see if the O is closed properly or not - this equates to someone's mouth being 'open' (talkative) or 'closed' (tight-lipped):

tight-lipped

talkative

very talkative

secretive

The last of these, 'secretive' shows an O with a loop in it - just imagine that this is someone 'biting their lip'.

It is very rare to get double loops (one each end) of an O, especially at the end of a short word such as 'two'. However, if you do see these it shows even more than biting of the lip - deceit!

The Letter E

With the letter E the size of the loop that creates the E represents the ability of someone to listen:

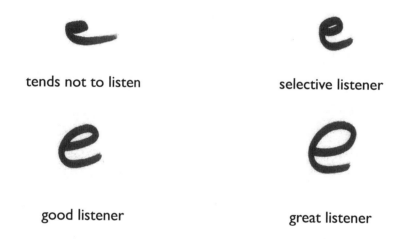

tends not to listen   selective listener

good listener   great listener

The letter E even looks like an ear when it is written down so it really couldn't be any easier to remember - is their ear open or closed?

Putting the O and E together

By looking at the O and the E at the same time you can quickly get an idea of the way someone communicates with other people. They could be great at listening but almost never talk, indicating someone who is a shoulder to cry on in times of need, but should to try harder to open themselves up to other people. Or they could be the opposite and never listen to a word anyone else says whilst talking the ear off of every person they meet.

Open O / Open E	A great talker and great listener, this person is very open and has great communication skills
Open O / Closed E	Talks a lot but is not a great listener so may spend a lot of the time talking over people
Closed O / Open E	Hardly says a word but makes a great listener, may be a great shoulder to cry on
Closed O / Closed E	Very quiet and introverted

This chart of course doesn't allow for the relative sizes of the letters and how open and closed they are - it's up to you to judge how much of each trait a person has by comparing bother letters together.

O & E Recap
The more open the O, the more they talk
The bigger the Earhole, the more they listen

Exercise Four

By looking at the O and the E ONLY, can you match these samples with their descriptions?

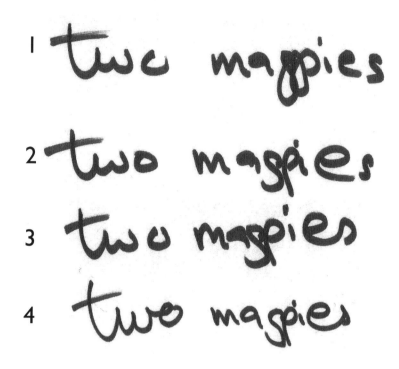

1   two magpies

2   two magpies

3   two magpies

4   two magpies

A - Good listener but doesn't give much away

B - Open and engaging

C - Quiet but good listener

D - Extremely talkative but doesn't listen to anyone else

5. A and S – Cats and Birds

The A and the S are the last remaining letters of our phrase and deal with relationships and attention seeking.

These letters have the least importance out of all the letters we have dealt with and as such have been left till last. That doesn't mean we can't have some fun with them though!

The Letter A

The letter A sometimes has a 'cat claw' to the left of it when it is written down, making it look somewhat like a letter C instead:

Normal A   'Cat's Claw' A

The claw comes from the way the A is drawn after coming from the previous letter (the M in our case). A's written on their own or at the start of words will seldom have this 'cat claw'.

When people draw an A with this 'claw', graphology sees this as the person having issues with the opposite sex. If this is the case, the kind of issues may become apparent from the other parts of the analysis.

> **Memory tip**: We all know when people are being 'Catty' - and the C and the A are the first two letters of CAT.

The Letter S

The letter S is the last letter of our phrase and gives us an idea of how much attention someone needs depending on the length of it's tail:

magpies

Normal S

magpies

Moderate attention seeking S

magpies

Extreme attention seeking S

The longer the tail, the more attention someone craves.

Memory tip: The S is the tail of our word 'magpies' and we all know how their tail feathers point up and catch our attention - as do that of peacocks and other birds.

28

Putting the A and S together

In all fairness it is quite rare to get the A claw and the S tail even once, let alone together. However if you do get one of them you have now done enough steps in the analysis to be able to see how these traits might apply.

For instance, if you have the 'claw' in the A, you could go back over the previous letters to figure out what kind of problems the person may have with the opposite sex. Women may have a strong physical presence as seen by the letter P which men may find a turn off. Men may have lofty ambitions and goals as seen by their T and I letters, showing an inability to be realistic in relationships with the opposite sex.

If someone has an attention seeking S, perhaps their waves (W) and mountains (M) are extremely jagged and sharp too, showing someone who pushes themselves for the adoration of others. Or perhaps they are fairly anti-social with a small G loop, which would show a conflict with their need for attention suggesting a fairly frustrated individual.

Looking over the previous traits with a healthy dose of common sense can unearth all kinds of information.

A & S Recap
C shape in the A = Catty with opposite sex
Tail on the magpies = craves attention

Exercise Five

By looking at the A and the S ONLY, can you match these samples with their descriptions?

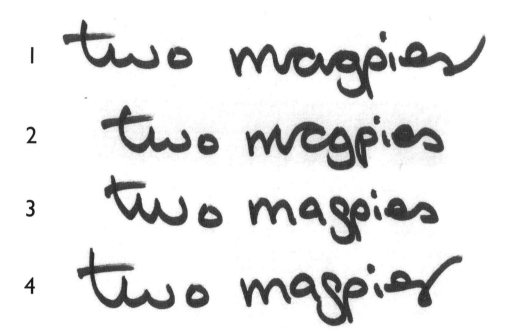

B -	Issues with opposite sex
A -	Tend to seek attention but has issues with opposite sex
D -	Needs attention
C -	Normal

Answers: 1B:2A:3D:4C

30

6. Slants and baselines

The slants and angles that people display in their hand-writing shows us their slants and angles on life.

Slants

The slant of someone's handwriting refers to the way the letters in a word or phrase appear to be leaning to the left or right. Most people's handwriting tends to lean somewhere between being perfectly upright or leaning slightly forward:

The more that the handwriting slants forwards and to the right, the more emotionally responsive someone is said to be:

The more that the handwriting slants backwards and to the left, the more emotionally withdrawn someone is said to be:

* ***Top Tip***: *It is very rare that someone's handwriting slants both to the left AND to the right over the course of a sentence or phrase. However, if you do see this rare occurrence it is seen to represent someone with a dual personality.*

Baselines

The baseline refers to an imaginary line drawn under the handwriting to enable us to judge the angle at which the handwriting rises up or down the page. This is extremely easy to spot in most cases, but if you are having trouble then it is a simple matter to imagine that the paper is lined horizontally and judge the handwriting from there.

Put simply, someone whose writing rises up the page has an upbeat optimistic character, and when the writing falls down the page they have a more pessimistic downbeat view of the world:

Straight baseline - Normal

Rising baseline - Upbeat

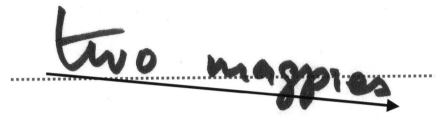

Falling baseline - Downbeat

Memory tip: Someone's angle on life is reflected in the rise and fall of their handwriting.

*** Top Tip**: *If someone's handwriting slants backwards it could well be that they are left-handed in which case this whole concept is reversed.*

*** Top Tip**: *Someone who has a wavy or uneven baseline could be rather up and down as you can imagine!*

Slants & Baselines Recap

Slants forward = leans towards you

Slants backward = leans away from you

Angled up = upbeat

Angled down = downbeat

Exercise Seven

By looking at the slants and baselines ONLY, can you match these samples with their descriptions?

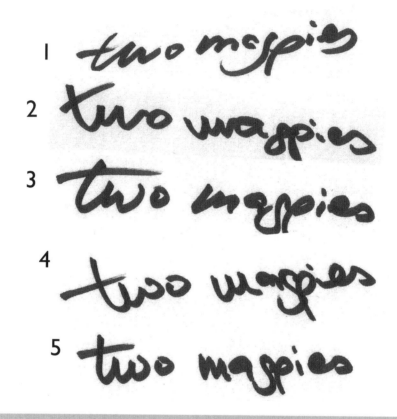

E - Well balanced

C - Well balanced and sociable

A - Open and upbeat

B - Dual personality mainly downbeat

D - Upbeat but somewhat reserved

7. Style

magpiES

Now it's time to take a look at the overall handwriting style of the individual

We've seen how the individual letters in our 'two magpies' phrase can give us a great insight into someone's character, and how the way their handwriting slants and pitches on the page can tell us even more about them. Now it's time to take a general overview of their unique style.

Unlike the other sections, there are fewer cut and dry rules you can apply to the overall style of someone's handwriting so it is easier to go through a checklist in your head of what you are actually looking for, and judge them accordingly.

There are six traits we are looking at in someone's handwriting style:

S	*Spacing*
C	*Connectivity*
R	*Regularity*
A	*Accuracy*
W	*Width*
L	*Large*

This leaves us with the acronym SCRAWL which is easy to remember. The last letter for 'Large' refers to size (small/large) of the handwriting.

35

S for Spacing

Look at the space between the words 'two' and 'magpies' - are the words widely separated or close together? The distance between the words shows how much distance the person puts between himself and others.

Loner

Forges close relationships

C for Connectivity

Here we are looking to see how much the letters of each word are joined up.

People with connected handwriting tend to be single minded
as their pen hardly leaves the page as they write

Disconnected handwriting shows a more creative, agile approach
as each letter is taken separately and given it's own space

Those that have a mixture of connected and joined up writing are able to see their creative ideas through into reality

R for Regularity

S	C	**R**	A	W	L

A quick glance at the two words and you can easily make this judgement.

Regular and controlled writing shows self-control

Irregular writing shows creative and irregular thoughts

A for Accuracy

S	C	R	**A**	W	L

Just because something is irregular doesn't mean it isn't accurate - the last two examples were both legible and the last one was accurate in it's own way.

Inaccurate writing and frequent 'fixing' of miss-formed letters can indicate learning difficulties

too magpys

People who have dyslexia often write very neatly
even thought their spelling is inaccurate

> ** Top Tip: Be very careful with what you say regarding people who's writing is miss-spelt or badly written. Some of the most ingenious thinkers are dyslexic and people with badly formed writing often excel in other areas. Highlight the positives and talk about the difficulties that arise from 'being different' without laboring the point too much.*

W For Width

| S | C | R | A | **W** | L |

The width of someone's handwriting shows us how broadly they think.

two magpies

Broad thinking, open minded, easy going

two magpies

Concentration, one thing at a time, focus

The size of a person's handwriting can show how outgoing and confident someone is and is a good indicator of modesty versus outspokenness.

Large handwriting shows an outgoing and confident person

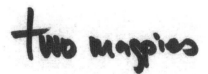

Very small writing shows a modest and precise individual

Style Recap
Use the SCRAWL acronym to remember the six steps to understanding overall style

Additional notes

This section is more open to interpretation than any other part of the analysis. The acronym *SCRAWL* is there so you don't forget anything, but with practice you are looking to make a fairly broad judgement of the person's overall style. If you get a 'hunch' about someone's handwriting i.e. it looks artistic / mechanical / girly etc then go with it. As you look at more samples of handwriting, try and go with your instincts and use *SCRAWL* to fall back on should you be lacking inspiration.

Exercise Eight

By looking at the style ONLY, can you match these samples with their descriptions?

1 two magpies

2 two magpies

3 two magpies

4 two magpies

5 two magpies

A - Single minded and focused

B - Generally pretty creative

C - Outgoing and confident, creative and easy going

D - Precise, focused and rather quiet

E - Creative loner

Answers: 1B:2C:3A:4E:5D

40

8. Signature

Harry Houdini

A signature can reveal a lot about someone's openness to other people and is their most personal of scribbles.

The signature of a person is of course their most personal scribble and can be used to add some extra details to the overall analysis.

Just like the writing of the phrase 'two magpies', the slant and baseline concepts all apply to the signature and it is rare to find one that doesn't reflect someone's overall handwriting style in some way.

What They Write

To begin with, simply ignore the style of the signature and take a look at the names they have written down. Have they used all their names, initials or a bit of both? The personal information someone reveals in their signature can be quite telling.

Someone who writes their full name is usually a person
who is steadfast and trustworthy

Someone who misses out their first name by using an initial is more
formal and less open about themselves

41

Harry

A signature that is simply someone's first name shows someone who is very open and informal, even flamboyant

Houdini

A surname only can show seriousness

When you think about it this is all common sense. A signature shows how someone projects themselves to the outside world and the way they use their first names or surnames reflects that.

How They Write It

The style in which someone actually writes their signature also tells us a fair bit about them. Just like their overall handwriting style, the rise or fall of a signature up and down the page can denote a positive or pessimistic attitude to life. However there are two more things to consider:

HH

Can you read it? - An illegible signature can show egotism
However, it can also be that of someone who signs their signature a lot

Houdini (signature)

Is it underlined? - An underlined signature can show a powerful character

A full stop at the end can show assertion.. People who write full stops at the end of their signatures can be quite powerful characters, although set in their ways.

*** Top Tip**: If there is a huge difference between some-one's general writing style and the style of their signature you have the makings of an interesting analysis - there is obviously some kind of inner conflict going on with the individual.*

<u>Signature Recap</u>
Check use of forenames/surnames
Check the baseline of the signature
and see if you can actually read what it says,
noticing any underlining or full stops

Exercise Nine

What can we say about these people in regards to their handwriting?

1 J. Moore

2 Jilian

3 Jilian Moore

4 *(signature)*

5 Moore

6 Jilian Moore

7 Jilian Moore

Answers: 1F;2B;3C;4E;5A;6G;7D

9. Putting It Into Practice

Now you've got the method you're ready to take your new found skills on the road.

The 'two magpies' method can be used in a couple of different ways. The most practical, and the one you will probably spend the most of your time using, is to simply have people write the two words and their signature down on the back of a business card or on a small pad of paper. It is entirely up to you whether you keep it light hearted and explain the method as you go or act the expert and keep your method hidden. I always teach the method as I go as people tend to remember it and try it on all their friends later.

However, 'two magpies' can be used as a memory aid for analysing almost any length of handwriting sample without even mentioning the phrase. In these cases 'two magpies' becomes an easy way to remember some of the most important elements to look for in someone's handwriting.

Using the method for a group of people in a light hearted fashion is one of it's best uses as it is very easy to explain the first five steps without having to see too much of the handwriting itself apart from answering the odd question. If you are doing graphology analysis for five people at a time then analysing the letters only may be all you need. Should you have a person who is more interested, more important or simply better looking then it's easy to just continue on to the other steps with them to one side.

ten magpies

Here are some other things to look out for to enhance your handwriting analysis

G & P

When the width of the G loop is very large it can indicate an extremely active sexual imagination

A G loop that cuts halfway across the downstroke can indicate a fear of success

Incomplete G loops can show physical frustration

- - - - - - - - - - - - -

T & I (Golf Analogy)

Hooked on the past
When the T is crossed with a 'hook' in the backswing, it can mean holding on to the past - someone's ability to move forward is hindered by not letting go

Reaching for the future
When the T is crossed with a 'hook' right out front it can show someone who is looking for new things and may be entrepreneurial

Dagger-like sarcasm
A T bar crossed which ends in a sharp point can denote sarcasm

- - - - - - - - - - - - -

M & W

W's with circle in them show a desire for responsibility

O & E

two

When there are two bitten 'lips' on the O it can mean lying

- - - - - - - - - - - -

Baselines

two magpies

When someone's handwriting rises and falls it shows someone
who is a good starter but bad finisher

two magpies

When someone's handwriting falls then rises it shows someone
who starts slow but enjoys finishing projects

*** Top Tip**: Remember right at the start we asked people
to write 'two magpies' in lower case? Well, some people
won't be paying attention and may well draw a capital T
at the beginning of 'two'. You now know something
about them immediately - they tend not to listen!*

49

Which Beatle are you?

A fun thing to do is to compare people's signatures to that of The Beatles. The four personality types are all quite different and it's interesting to see if someone's handwriting actually matches up with which Beatle they *think* they are.

11. Analysis Samples

Here we take a look at some real world samples to show how an short analysis may develop

<u>**Sample A**</u>

GP - Fear of success, not a particularly physical person
(G loop cuts halfway through stem. P has no loop)

TI - Enthusiastic but tends to go too far, perhaps compensating for the past
(High T bar shows positive outlook, dot of the I has overshot indicating trying too hard, small hook at the back of the T bar shows holding on to the past)

WM - Able to switch between fairly broad and precise thinking, diplomatic
(W looks like normal waves in contrast to the pinnacles of the M, and the M slopes down)

OE - Extremely chatty and open and a good listener
(O is very open indeed and the E has a nice clean loop to it)

AS - Normal

Slants - Normal but has slight withdrawn tendency
(The 'two' is slanting backwards as is the 'm' of magpies)

Baselines - generally upbeat

(The phrase rises slightly)

Style / Spacing - Normal

Style / Connectivity - Quite creative and able to think in different ways
(A mixture of connected and unconnected letters)

Style / Regularity - Fairly regular, normal

Style / Accuracy - Normal, but some indication of awkwardness
(The w of 'two' is rather inaccurate)

Style / Width - Concentration
(The style isn't that wide)

Style / Large (Size) - Detail and precision
(The writing is quite small)

Signature / Names Used - Fairly formal
(Doesn't use first name)

Signature / Other - Assertive
(Full stop at the end)

I can see that you are not a particularly physical person, and you like people to a certain extent. There seems to be a tendency for you to shun success which is surprising as you have a lot of enthusiasm. Perhaps you are compensating for the past in some way. You have the ability to switch between from fairly broad projects to those that require a lot more precision. You certainly seem to be diplomatic, and this is enhanced by your ability to be a good listener, but sometimes you may have a tendency to talk just a little too much. This may be to make up for the fact that you are not a natural with people and tend to be slightly guarded. You have a generally upbeat nature, quietly creative and once again I see other tendencies in your handwriting indicating the ability to see the large and the smaller picture - yours is an agile mind. There is some awkwardness however and once again from your signature you make up for this with an assertive attitude for your own protection.

Sample B

GP-Fairly gregarious not particularly physical
(Good loop on the G none on the P)

TI - Optimistic and uses experience to good use
(High T crossing with slight back hook and accurate dot on the I - however it does seem rather 'busy' where the T is crossed so this could be a tendency to procrastinate)

WM - Easy going and open, quick thinking
(Nice curvy W, quite jagged M)

OE - Secretive, selective listener
(Loop in the O, fairly small E loop)

AS - Normal

Slants - Engaging
(Slightly leaning forward handwriting)

Baselines - Upbeat
(Writing lightly rises up the page)

Style / Spacing - Loner
(Words are not just written far apart but on different lines)

Style / Connectivity - Fluid thinker
(A mixture of joined up and separate letters)

Style / Regularity - Regular, normal

Style / Accuracy - Regular, normal

Style / Width - Focused
(Quite thin writing)

Style / Large (Size) - Concentration
(Small writing)

Signature / Names Used - Fairly formal
(Doesn't use first name)

Signature / Other - Quite stubborn / powerful character
(Strongly underlined signature)

From your handwriting I notice a gregarious nature - you feel comfortable in the company of other people. However, this will be just general socialising and probably not a physical group pursuit. You have an optimistic nature and you put your previous life experiences to good use and tend to get what you want. You are easy going and think on your feet, but you do have a more secretive quieter side and have a tendency to drift off when other people are talking. Here we see a contradiction in your handwriting as some traits single you out as a loner. Perhaps there's a part of you that some people will never see. You are an agile thinker with a great ability to concentrate and focus on the task in hand, but you are quite formal in your approach with others, and can come across as stubborn at times. Some people may even find you slightly intimidating.

Sample C

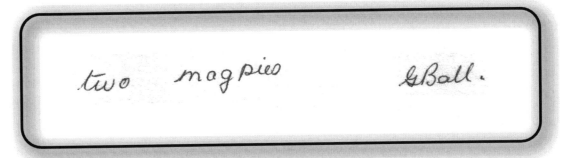

GP - Normal

TI - Level headed and forward thinking, accurate
(T crossed over to the right, accurate dot on i)

WM - Normal broad thinking
(Curvy W and M)

OE - Fairly quiet
(Closed O and hardly open E)

AS - Normal

Slants - Normal

Baselines - Optimistic
(Gently rising baseline)

Style / Spacing - Moderate loner
(Both words slightly more apart than usual)

Style / Connectivity - Creative thinker
(Mixed joined and disconnected handwriting)

Style / Regularity - Normal

Style / Accuracy - Precise

Style / Width - Normal

Style / Large (Size) - Concentration and accuracy
(All the letters are very small and precise)

Signature / Names Used - Formal
(No first name, again a very precise signature)

Signature / Other - Stubborn
(Full stop at end of signature)

You are a very level headed individual and you seem to pay attention to details. You have a broad outlook on life, and you are happy on the whole, although you do tend to keep yourself to yourself - some people may even call you shy. You have an active and creative mind and your precise nature, although natural, must come in useful. You tend to be quite formal and like to follow the rules, but this can make you quite stubborn.

* Top Tip: If you are finding it difficult to say much about a person's handwriting, then this in itself is revealing - if you can't make much from their handwriting then most people aren't going to be able to make much of them either! When this is the case, revert to other clues such as what they are wearing, their demeanor and suchlike. This may help you a great deal.

Sample D

GP - Quite gregarious
(Large G loop)

TI - Strong outlook, looking to the future
(High T bar, slight hook at the end, accurate dot on the I)

WM - Well balanced steady thinking
(Curvy W and M - extremely curvy M could suggest creativity)

OE - Fairly quite but good listener
(Closed O, open E)

AS - Normal

Slants - Lightly reserved
(Very light backwards slant)

Baselines - Normal / Controlled
(Phrase and signature are both very straight showing control)

Style / Spacing - Normal

Style / Connectivity - Agile thinker
(Mix of connected and disconnected letters)

Style / Regularity - Normal

Style / Accuracy - Normal

Style / Width - Normal

Style / Large (Size) - Normal

Signature / Names Used - Formal
(Uses abbreviated first name)

Signature / Other - Strong character
(*At first this could be seen as someone trying to 'cross out' their own name, which can show dissatisfaction with oneself - however, if you look closely the broad sweep serves to cross the two Ts in the name*)

> You are quite a people loving person with a strong outlook - you have a steady head on your shoulders and look forward to the future. Your slightly reserved nature means you tend to be quiet but are a good listener. Your level handwriting shows you keep your emotions in check, and this belies the fact that there is an active brain ticking away in there planning your next move. You have a strong and assertive nature, and like things to be just so.

*** Top Tip**: Finding contradictory traits is a good thing as you can show how one trait compensates another. This is true for all kinds of readings, and is why doing things in pairs always makes your life easier.*

Sample E

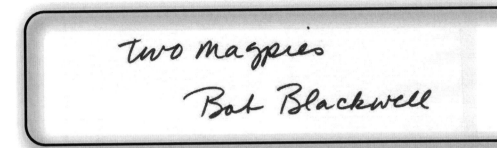

GP - Gregarious, not that physically inclined
(Nice G loop. no P loop)

TI - High enthusiasm with slightly less follow-through, often over stretches himself
(High crossed T bar slightly more to the left than right, dot of the I a fair bit past the stem of the I)

WM -Well balanced and diplomatic
(Wavy W and curvy M, slight downwards slant on the M)

OE - Fairly quiet, not a great listener
(Closed O, closed E)

AS -Normal

Slants - Quite open
(Slants gently to the right)

Baselines - Pretty upbeat
(Handwriting slopes gently upwards)

Style / Spacing -Normal

Style / Connectivity - Single minded
(Handwriting is pretty much connected throughout)

Style / Regularity -Normal
(However, it's very regular in it's own artistic way)

Style / Accuracy - Normal

Style / Width - Normal

Style / Large (Size) -Precision
(The writing is quite small and neat)

Signature / Names Used - Open, trustworthy
(Uses both names in the signature)

Signature / Other - Normal

You are a people person with a highly creative streak. *(I'm saying this because the handwriting just kind of looks cool!)* You have great enthusiasm for everything you do, but sometimes try to do too many things at once which can lead to procrastination - sometimes you can't make your mind up which thing to start next! You have a well balanced nature and are ever the diplomat - however, you could do with listening a bit more. You are single minded in your approach to life, and your precise handwriting shows someone who pays strict attention to detail. You are a very open and trustworthy individual and are well liked.

*** Top Tip**: If you get a hunch about someone's writing being 'cool', 'interesting' or 'artistic' go with it - you are probably right.*

12. A Final Note

As you may have noticed, this book is not called 'Graphology For The Metropolitan Police' or 'The N.Y.P.D. Bible Of Handwriting Analysis'. As such you should look at the material covered in this book as a quick way to get started with handwriting analysis so you can offer a fun and entertaining diversion to a group of friends or an audience of eager participants who would enjoy a bit of light hearted fun.

If someone is asking for your advice on whether so-and-so's scribble looks like the handwriting of a guy who might be having an affair with their wife then I would refer them to someone who works in forensic graphology. Only then offering to analyse their own handwriting for a small fee in a vain attempt to cheer them up.

Saying that, the ideas in this book are largely accurate regarding modern handwriting analysis. The only thing that could be considered a slight deviation from the norm is the Golf Analogy, but even that is pretty much the same as you will read in any other modern graphology book regarding the letter T.

Hopefully this book has got you up to speed in a very short time. By using the 'two magpies' phrase you are always good to go and just like palmistry, you'll be amazed how much people like to be told things about themselves!

Good luck, and may Two Magpies bring you lots of joy!

Julian Moore

FURTHER READING

Two books that have been invaluable during the course of writing this book have been 'Handwriting Analysis: The Art And Science Of Reading Character By Grapho Analysis' by M.N. Bunker and 'Handwriting Analysis Dictionary' by Lorraine Owens.

The Bunker book is an old 1959 book which is out of date in it's writing style, but filled full of examples and was one of the first books about graphology that I ever got my hands on.

The 'Handwriting Analysis Dictionary' is another out of print book written in the 80's by this high-profile graphologist. It was published by her own company and is an exhaustive A-Z of all the handwriting traits. If you are serious about taking graphology a step further, start hunting for this book right away.

ADDENDUM

In my book 'Palm Reading In Your Own Words' I discuss the merits of finding contradictory traits in the hand. For those of you that don't have the book, here is the section that deals with this, copied here for sake of completeness. The concept works with any kind of reading, and is one of the reasons I grouped the letters of my graphology method into pairs. I have changed the word 'hand' to the word 'handwriting' where applicable.

CONTRADICTIONS ARE GOOD FOR YOU

As you try to create useful readings from these practice tests, you may find that even though you thought that having sets of traits which were complimentary were much easier to talk about, quite the opposite is true.

These traits:

Healthy / Down to earth / Adaptable / Practical hard working

are so complimentary they almost cancel themselves out! They all point to the same thing, and don't really tell you much about the person that you couldn't have easily found out about already. You will find that although it's good to discover the commonalities in a persons handwriting, it's the *differences* which yield the most interesting information.

The set of traits above show someone who's a nice, hard working but easy going kind of guy. When you simply change one of the traits thus:

Healthy / Down to earth / **Inflexible** / Practical hard working

you have a lot more to go on as you now have something that could be perceived as *negative* in the mix. This set of traits shows someone who's a hard working kind of guy who needs to avoid being set in his ways and see the bigger picture. There is something more interesting to say simply because *Adaptable* was changed to *Inflexible*.

It's very nice when someone's handwriting shows a lot of similar traits as it defines them more quickly, but it doesn't really help you give them any advice. As a reader you are not only telling people what they are like, but what to watch out for - some of the pitfalls in their personality which could hinder their progress and they should be made aware of.

Without differences and conflicts you will have very little to tell someone, so you need to bring up the differences at every opportunity. That is why is it good to scan their handwriting and find at least two conflicting traits each time you want to speak.

You can start by describing an undesirable trait and then back it up with a good one:

> 'Although you have trouble keeping your energy levels up, you are able to compensate for this with your resilient nature'

or you could do it the other way around:

> 'You are able to switch from one task to another effortlessly but are easily distracted from the matter in hand when something more appealing shows up'

Switching between these two modes of communication is extremely effective and keeps the reading flowing.

Printing & Technical

Download / Flash Cards

This ebook comes with another PDF document containing the ten flash cards that you can use to learn the method.

You can download when you register this book at:

http://thecoldreadingcompany.co.uk/coldreading/gflash

They have been designed to print onto index cards which measure 4 inches by 6 inches (10.16 cm X 15.24 cm).

The easiest way I have found to do this is:

First:

• Choose 4X6 in the print menu when choosing paper size
• Make sure the print preferences are set to 'landscape'

Then:

• Put 5 blank index cards in the printer short side in
• Print pages 1-10 with 'odd pages only' selected
• When those are printed, take them out together and place them back into the printer feeder blank side out ready for printing again
• Print pages 1-10 with 'even pages only' selected

And then:

• Repeat with another 5 blank cards for pages 11-20
Doing 5 cards at a time front and back is a lot easier than doing ten at a time!

Audiobook

You can download the audiobook that accompanies this text from the website:

http://thecoldreadingcompany.co.uk

BY THE SAME AUTHOR

DON'T JUST **TELL** THEM ABOUT IT ~
LEAVE THEM WITH A SOUVENIR!

TO BE USED IN CONJUNCTION WITH THE ORIGINAL 'SPEED LEARNING
GRAPHOLOGY - THE ART OF HANDWRITING ANALYSIS' BOOK

≈Speed Learning
GRAPHOLOGY

THE SPEED LEARNING GRAPHOLOGY
COMPANION SYSTEM

 &

**INSTRUCTION
BOOKLET**

**GRAPHOLOGY
'TICK SHEET'**

A BEAUTIFUL 'GREETINGS CARD' STYLE FORMAT
YOUR FRIENDS AND CLIENTS WILL LOVE

FOOLPROOF MEMORY SYSTEM ~ NEVER MISS A THING
~ CREATE A UNIQUE MOMENTO THEY'LL KEEP FOREVER!

ADD YOUR DETAILS ~PRINT THEM OUT
SPREAD YOUR NAME!

JULIAN MOORE

INCLUDES GRAPHICS TEMPLATES AND INSTRUCTION MANUAL

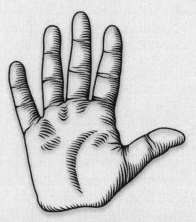

BY THE SAME AUTHOR

BY THE SAME AUTHOR

71

Made in the USA
Monee, IL
03 October 2021

79256296R10042